Nietzsche on Love

Warbler Press

ISBN 978-1-7344525-7-0 (paperback)
ISBN 978-1-7344525-8-7 (e-book)

warblerpress.com

Warbler Press Contemplations current and forthcoming titles at warblerpress.com

Nietzsche on Love

Friedrich Nietzsche

EDITED AND TRANSLATED BY ULRICH BAER

Contents

Nietzsche on Love

Wanting to be loved. The demand to be loved is the greatest presumption of all.

Whatever is done out of love always takes place beyond good and evil.

It is true: we love life not because we are used to living but because we are used to loving.

This is what is most difficult: to close one's open hand out of love and to maintain one's shame as someone who gives.

What else is love but to understand and to rejoice in the fact that another person lives, acts, and feels in a way that is different from and opposed to ours? If love is to bridge these oppositions through joy, it must not overcome or deny them.—Even self-love contains the unblendable duality (or multitude) in one person as its precondition.

One day you shall love beyond yourselves! So first learn to love! And that is why you had to drink the bitter cup of your love. There is bitterness even in the best love…

A craving for love is in me that itself speaks the language of love.

And often with our love we only want to leap over envy.

Thus speaks all great love: it overcomes even forgiveness and pity.

You too love the earth and the earthly: I have divined you well!—but shame and a bad conscience is in your love. In this you are like the moon.

Loving and perishing, these two go together from eternity. The will to love: that means also to be willing to die.

But I lay chained to the love for my children. Desire had laid this trap for me, this desire for love, so that I would become my children's prey and lose myself to them.

Never in my life have I groveled before the mighty; and if I ever lied, I lied for love.

All great love does not want love:—it wants more.

Where one can no longer love there one should—
move along!

Finally his heart was transformed—and one morning he [Zarathustra] rose with the dawn, stepped before the sun, and spoke to him thus: "You mighty star! What would your happiness be if you did not have those for whom you shine!"

What is great about the human is that he is a bridge and not a goal: what can be loved in the human is that he is a transition and a decline.

Long love—even when it is happy—is possible because a human being is not easily possessed all the way to the end, not easily conquered all the way to the end. There are always new, yet undiscovered depths and hidden chambers that open in the soul, and love's unending greed reaches even for those.— But love ends as soon as we experience the person to be limited.

A male illness. The safest way of guarding against the male illness of self-contempt is to be loved by an intelligent woman.

The more people know themselves to be loved, the more ruthless they frequently become until they are no longer worthy of love, and a rift actually appears.

A testament to love. Someone said: "I have never thoroughly thought about two people: this is a testament of my love for them."

The deepest insights are gained only out of love.

What you have called the world should first be created by you: your reason, your image, your willpower, your love it should become!

The noblest of drives
Ennoble with intent:
For every pound of love
An ounce of self-contempt!

Now it is nighttime: now all rushing fountains speak more loudly. And my soul is a rushing fountain as well.

Now it is nighttime: only now all the lover's songs awaken. And my soul is a lover's song as well.

And let my stream of love plunge into impassable terrain! How should a torrent not find its way to the sea at last! There is a secluded and self-sufficient lake inside of me; but the current of my love pulls it downward alongside it—to the ocean!

The fire of love and the fire of anger glow in the names of all virtues.

Economy of goodness.—Goodness and love as the most salutary medicines in human conduct are such precious discoveries that one would wish for these balms to be used as economically as possible: but this is impossible. The economy of goodness is the dream of the most audacious utopians.

One can promise actions but not feelings, because those are involuntary. When someone promises another person to love them forever, hate them forever, or be faithful forever, he promises something not in his power. Surely he can promise such actions, which are usually the consequences of love, hatred, and loyalty, but they can also be based on other motives since several different ways and motives can lead to the same action. The promise to love someone forever therefore means: As long as I love you, I will render to you the actions of love. When I no longer love you, you will continue to receive the same actions from me, but now based on other motives so that in the minds of other people the impression remains that love is unchanged and still the same.—One therefore promises the continuation of the appearance of love when one swears without self-deception everlasting love to someone.

Love and justice.—Why do we overestimate love when compared to justice and say the most wonderful things about it, as if it were of a far higher nature that the latter? Is love not recognizably more stupid than justice?—Certainly, but precisely for this reason it is so much more *pleasant* for everyone. It is stupid and endowed with a rich cornucopia from which it bestows its gifts to anyone, even when that person does not deserve it and does not even thank it for them. It is impartial like the rain which, according to the Bible and based on experience, soaks to the skin not only the unjust man but, possibly, also the just.

Honor transferred from the person to the thing.—One generally honors the actions of love and the sacrifices for those nearest to us, wherever they may appear. This increases the *value of the things* that are loved in this way or for which one sacrifices oneself, even though by themselves they might not be worth very much. A brave army makes the cause for which it fights convincing.

Marriage as a long conversation.—When entering into a marriage one should ask oneself this question: do you believe that you will have good conversations with this woman up into old age? Everything else in a marriage is transitory, but most of the time you will spend together will involve conversation.

Marriage: this is what I call the will of two individuals to create one thing that is more than those who created it. Reverence before one another: that is what I call marriage as before those individuals who want such a will. This ought to be the meaning and truth of your marriage. But that which the all-too-many and the superfluous ones call marriage,—alas, what do I call that? Ah, this poverty of soul between two people! Ah, this filth of soul between two people! Ah, this pathetic comfort between two people!

All this they call marriage; and they say their marriages are made in Heaven. Well, I do not like it, this Heaven of the superfluous! No, I do not like them, these animals caught in the heavenly net! And the God who limps along to bless what he did not join, he would also stay distant from me! Do not laugh at such marriages! Which child would not have reason to cry over its parents?

Whoever praises him as a God of Love does not hold love in high enough esteem. Did this God not also want to be a judge? But the lover loves beyond recompense and retaliation.

And be on your guard against the onslaughts of your love! The lonely person extends his hand too quickly to anyone he encounters.

The spiritualizing of sensuality is called love.

Love is the condition in which man sees things most decidedly in a way they are not. The power of illusion is at its height there, just as the power to sweeten and transfigure things. When in love, man endures more than at any other time; he submits to anything.

Love for another person is barbarism: for it is carried out at the expense of all others. Even the love for God.

The value of the belief in superhuman passions.—The institution of marriage stubbornly maintains the belief that love, although a passion, can be made permanent, and that permanent, life-long *love* can be posited as a rule. By means of this noble and tenacious belief, even though it is contradicted so often and almost as a rule, which makes it a *pia fraus* [pious fraud], marriage has elevated love to a higher rank. All institutions that have conceded to passion the belief in its duration and our responsibility for this duration, the nature of passion notwithstanding, have raised passion to a higher status. Anyone now experiencing such a passion no longer considers himself, as in earlier times, humiliated or threatened by it but elevated before himself and his equals. Let us recall institutions and customs which, out of the fiery devotion of a moment, have created eternal fidelity; out of the pleasure of anger, eternal vengeance; out of despair, eternal mourning; out of a single hasty word, eternal obligation. A great deal of hypocrisy and falsehood has come into the world as the result of such transformations; but each time, too, at this cost, a new and *superhuman* conception which elevates mankind.

But even your best love is only a passionate compari-
son and a painful ardor. It is a torch that should light
your way to higher paths.

There is always some madness in love. But there is also always some reason in madness.

Now I love God: humans I do not love. The human is too imperfect a thing for me. Love of mankind would kill me.

The degree and type of a person's sexuality reaches up into the uppermost peaks of their spirit.

The cause of "altruism."—People have always spoken of *love* with such emphasis and divine adoration because until now they have *experienced little of it* and were never permitted to get their fill of it: so it became the "food of the gods" for them. If a poet were to show in a utopian vision the universal *love for other humans* as an actual occurrence, he would certainly have to describe an agonizing and pitiful state of things never before seen on earth,—everyone adored, chased, and desired not by a single lover, as may happen today, but by thousands and indeed by everyone, as the result of an uncontrollable drive, which would then be maligned and cursed in the same way as selfishness had been in the past. The poets who describe this condition, if they were granted enough leisure to imagine this, would dream up nothing but this blissful and loveless past filled with divine selfishness and the then still existing possibilities on earth of being by oneself, undisturbed, unloved, hated and despised, or whatever else we call the baseness of the beautiful animal world in which *we* live.

Finally this vilification of Eros has taken a comedic turn: The "devil" Eros has gradually become more interesting for humans than all the angels and saints, thanks to the obfuscation and secrecy of the church in all erotic matters.

Marriage in the *bourgeois* sense of the word, which means in the most respectable sense of the word "marriage," is not at all a matter of love, just as it is not a matter of money; no institution can be founded on love. It is a matter of society's granting permission to two people to gratify their sexual desire with one another under certain conditions, to be sure, but such conditions that keep in view the *interests of society*. It is obvious that a certain attraction among the participants and very much good will—will to patience, compatibility, care for one another—is among the preconditions for such a contract; but one should not misuse the word love to describe this! For two lovers in the complete and strong sense of the word, sexual gratification is nothing essential and really no more than a symbol; for one party, as mentioned, it is a symbol of unconditional submission, for the other a symbol of their consent, a sign of taking possession.—In marriage in the truly aristocratic sense it was a question of breeding a race (is there still an aristocracy today? One asks)—thus of the maintenance of a fixed, definite type of ruling men: man and woman were sacrificed to this point of view. It is obvious that love was not the first requirement here, on the contrary! and not even this modicum of good will for one another that is a condition of the good bourgeois marriage. A family's interest was the deciding factor and, above that, class. We would shiver a little at the coldness, severity and calculating clarity of such a noble concept of marriage that has ruled every healthy aristocracy, in ancient Athens and still in Europe of the eighteenth century, we warm-blooded animals with sensitive hearts, we "moderns!" Precisely this is why love as passion, in that word's expansive meaning, was *invented* for and in the aristocratic world, where compulsion and privation were greatest...

It is not the strength but the duration of a high sensation that makes high men.

A soul that knows itself to be loved but does not itself love exposes its sediment:—its lowest parts rise to the top.

Learning to love.—One has to learn to love and to be kind from an early age. If education and chance offer us no opportunities to practice these sensations, our soul will turn dry and unsuitable for understanding these tender inventions of lovely individuals. Hatred must also be learned and nourished if one wants to become a solid hater: otherwise the germ for it will gradually also wither and die.

Love.—Love forgives the beloved even his lust.

All the things called love.—Greed and love: what different feelings these terms evoke! And yet it could be the same drive, named twice: once denigrated by those who already own something and in whom the drive has quieted down a bit and who now fear for their "possessions," and the other time from the position of the unsatisfied, thirsty ones who therefore glorify it as "good." Love thy neighbor—is it not the craving for new *property*? And likewise our love of knowledge, of truth and in fact this craving of ours for anything new? We gradually grow tired of anything that is old and which we safely own, and stretch out our hands again. Even the most beautiful landscape is no longer assured of our love once we have lived in it for three months, at which point some more distant coast excites our cravings: possession usually diminishes what is possessed. The pleasure we take in ourselves tries to maintain itself by constantly transforming itself into something new *inside of us*—that is what ownership is called. To grow tired of something you own means: to grow tired of yourself. (You can suffer from too much—even the desire to throw things out and give them away can assume the noble name of "love.") When we see someone suffering, we like to use this opportunity to take possession of him. This is, for example, what charitable and compassionate people do, and they also name the desire for new possessions which has now arisen in them "love," and experience it like the kind of pleasure aroused by the prospect of a new conquest. But most clearly sexual love betrays itself as the craving for property: the lover wants the unconditional and sole possession of the longed-for person. He wants power over their soul that is as unconditional as his power over their body, he wants to be the only beloved, and to reside and rule in the other's soul as that which is highest and most desirable. Once you consider that this means nothing else but to *exclude* the whole world from a precious good, fortune and enjoyment, once you consider that the lover aims to impoverish and deprive all of his competitors and to become the dragon of his golden hoard as the most ruthless and selfish of all "conquerors" and exploiters: once you consider, finally, that to the lover the whole other world seems indifferent, pale and worthless and he is willing to make any sacrifice, disturb any order and subordinate any interest, then one wonders indeed that this wild greed and injustice of sexual love has been glorified and deified in this way through the ages. That from this type of love one has taken the concept of love as the opposite to selfishness when it may well be the most unabashed expression of selfishness. Here it has been clearly the have-nots and desirous ones who have invented our language use—there probably have always been too many of them. Those blessed with much property and satisfaction in this area may have uttered the occasional word of a "furious demon," like the most endearing and beloved of all Atheneans, Sophocles. But Eros has always laughed at such blasphemers—they were always especially his most beloved favorites.—Here and there on earth there may be a kind of continuation of love in which the greedy craving of two people successively yielded to a new desire and greed, a *shared* higher thirst for an ideal above them. But who knows this love? Who has experienced it? Its proper name is *friendship*.

On loving thy neighbor.—You crowd around those nearest to you and have beautiful words for it. But I say to you: your love for your neighbors is your bad love for yourself.

You are fleeing to the nearest and away from yourselves, and you want to turn this into a virtue: but I can see through your "selflessness."

The You is older than the I; the You has been made holy but not yet the I: thus man pushes himself toward the nearest one.

Do I recommend to you to love thy neighbor? I will rather recommend to you to flee thy neighbor and love those farthest away!

Higher than love for thy neighbor is the love for the most remote and for what is yet to come: even higher than love for other people is the love for things and ghosts.

This ghost that walks ahead of you, my brother, is more beautiful than you. Why don't you give him your flesh and your bones? But you are afraid and run to the nearest one.

You can't stand being with yourselves and do not sufficiently love yourselves. Now you want to seduce the nearest to love and to gild yourselves with his error.

I wish that you would be unable to stand being with all those nearby things and their neighbors. Then you would have to create your friend and his overflowing heart out of yourselves.

You invite a witness when you want to speak well of yourselves, and once you have seduced him to think well of you, you yourselves think well of yourselves.

It is not only he who speaks against what he knows who is a liar, but especially he who speaks against what he does not know. And so you speak of yourselves when dealing with others and lie to the neighbor with yourselves.

So the fool says: "Being among people corrupts one's characters, especially when you have none."

One runs to his neighbor because he is looking for himself, and another one does so because he wants to lose himself. Your bad love for yourselves turns solitude into a prison for you.

The more remote ones pay for your love for the neighbor; and when five of you have gathered together, a sixth one always has to die.

I also do not love your festivals because I found too many actors there and even the spectators behaved often like actors, too.

I don't teach you the nearest but the friend. The friend ought to be the festival of the earth and a premonition of the Over-man for you.

I teach you the friend and his overflowing heart. But you must understand how to be a sponge if you want to be loved by an overflowing heart.

I teach you the friend in whom the world stands completed, a vessel of goodness,—the creative friend who always has a completed world to give away.

And just as the world unravels for him it comes back together in circles—as good emerges from evil and goals emerge from coincidence.

The future and what is most remote ought to be the cause for your Today: in your friend you should love the Over-man as your cause.

My brothers, I do not exhort you to love thy neighbor: I exhort you to love the one who is farthest away.

Thus spoke Zarathustra.

Solitary man, you are going the way of the lover: you love yourself and for that reason you despise yourself the way only lovers can despise.

What is forgiven only with the greatest difficulty: respecting oneself. Such a being is simply abominable, because he brings to the surface what is truly the case with tolerance, the only virtue of the others and everyone...

I wish one would begin by *respecting* oneself: everything else follows from that. To be sure, as soon as one does *this* one is finished for the others: for this is what they forgive last: "What? A man who respects himself?"—

This is something different from the blind drive to *love* oneself: nothing is more common, in the love of the sexes as well as of that duality which is called "I," than *contempt* for what one loves:—fatalism in love.

Let there be bravery in your love! With your love you should attack whoever inspires fear in you! In your love should be your honor! Woman understands little besides this about honor. But this ought to be your honor, to always love more than you are being loved, and to never be second in this.

Man ought to fear woman when she loves: then she will make any sacrifice and any other thing seems without value for her.

Amor fati [love of fate]: let that be my *love* from now on! I do not want to wage war against ugliness. I do not want to accuse, I do not even want to accuse the accusers. Let looking away be my only form of denial! And, all in all and on the whole: at some point I want only to be a Yes-Sayer!

In every kind of female love some part of maternal love also comes to the fore.

Every great love brings with it the cruel thought to kill the object of love so that it may be removed once and for all from the wicked game of change: for love dreads change more than destruction.

Forbidden generosity.—There is not enough love and goodness in the world to give any of it away to conceited individuals.

Whoever directs his passion at things (science, politics, culture, arts) withdraws much fire from his passion for other people.

Friends in need.—Occasionally we notice that one of our friends belongs more to another than to us, that his sensitivity suffers because of this decision and his self-absorption does not suffice to act on it: then we must make things easier for him by *insulting* him *away* from us.—This is also necessary in cases when we begin to think in ways that would be detrimental for him: our love for him ought to compel us, by means of an injustice that we take upon ourselves, to create a good conscience for him in breaking with us.

Friends as ghosts.—When we undergo a powerful change, those of our friends who have not changed turn into ghosts of our own past: their voice sounds strange and shadow-like to our ears—as if we heard ourselves, but younger, harder, less mature.

Forcing oneself to pay attention.—As soon as we notice that someone has to *force* himself to pay attention when engaging and talking with us, we have absolute proof that he does not or no longer loves us.

Friend.—Experiencing joy together, not pain, makes the friend.

In the end, one loves one's desire, and not what one desires.

Love.—This subtlest artifice that Christianity has over the other religions is one word: it spoke of *love*. Thus it became the lyrical religion (while in its two other creations the Semitic culture bestowed heroic-epic religions upon the world). In the word love there is something so ambiguous and suggestive which speaks to memory and hope that even the lowest intelligence and the coldest heart feels something of the shimmer of this word. The most intelligent woman and the most common man think of the relatively least selfish moments of their whole life, even if Eros had barely lifted them up at any point, and those countless individuals whom love *passes by*, of parents, children or lovers, but especially those men and women who sublimated their sexuality, find their home in Christianity.

Deception in Love. We forget a good deal of our past and intentionally strike it from our minds: that is to say, we want our image that shines upon us from our past to lie to us and flatter our vanity,— we incessantly work on this self-deception.—And now you think, you who talk so much about and praise the "forgetting of oneself in love" and the "fusion of the I with the other person," that this is something essentially different? You shatter the mirror, fantasize your way into another person you admire and now take pleasure in the new image of yourselves, even if you call this by the other person's name—and this whole process is *not* supposed to be self-deception, *not* self-obsession! You are strange indeed!—I think that those who hide something about themselves *from themselves* and those who hide themselves in their entirety from themselves, are the same in that they commit a *theft* in the treasure chamber of understanding: from which we can see against what kind of transgression the sentence "know thyself" warns us.

The good friendship.—A good friendship originates when one person respects the other very much and, in fact, more than one's self, when one person also loves the other but not as much as one's self, and when finally, in order to facilitate the interaction, one knows how to add the tender *gloss* and down of intimacy while at the same time wisely refraining from actual and genuine intimacy and the confounding of I and You.

The source of great love.—What is the source of the deep and inner passions that a man suddenly experiences for a woman? Least of all sensuality alone: but when the man encounters in another person weakness, a need for help and exuberance all at once, something happens within him as if his soul would overflow: he is in the same instant moved and offended. At this point originates the source of great love.

A full and powerful soul not only copes with painful, even terrible losses, deprivations, robberies, insults; it emerges from such hells even vaster and more powerfully; and, to make the most essential point, with a new increase in the bliss of love. I believe that he who has grasped something of the lowest conditions for any increase in love will understand what Dante meant when he wrote over the gate of his Inferno: "I, too, was created by eternal love."

To be misunderstood.—When you are being misunderstood as a whole, it is impossible to completely correct being misunderstood in any particular instance. We have to recognize that in order not to squander excess energy in our defense.

Love.—The cult of love that women create is in essence and originally an invention of their intelligence, insofar as women increase their power through all of those idealizations of love and present themselves as ever more desirable in the eyes of men. But after getting used to this exaggerated estimation of love over the centuries, it has come to pass that they have run into their own net and forgotten this origin. Now they are even more deceived than men, and that is why women also suffer more from the disappointment that almost inevitably enters into every woman's life—as far as she has sufficient imagination and intelligence at all to be deceived and disappointed.

Friendship and Marriage.—The best friend will probably end up marrying the best spouse because a good marriage rests on the talent for friendship.

Love marriages.—Marriages that are entered into out of love (so-called marriages of love) have error for a father and hardship (need) for a mother.

The Unity of Place and Drama.—If spouses would not live together, better marriages would be more frequent.

Against the waste of love.—Do we not blush when we catch ourselves in a state of violent aversion? But we ought to feel the same in a state of violent attraction, on account of the injustice contained in them! Indeed: there are people who feel their hearts to be constrained and constricted when someone bestows his affection only in a manner that *deprives* others of this affection at the same time. When we hear in someone's tone of voice that *we* have been chosen and preferred! Alas, I am not grateful for being thus elected: I realize that I resent the other who wants to distinguish me in this way—he shall not love me at the *expense* of others! I am already busy enough to endure myself by myself! And frequently my heart is overflowing and I have reason to be joyful—and someone who has all of that should be given nothing that *others* so bitterly need!

To want to fall in love.—Couples who are engaged and have been brought together by utility frequently try to fall in love, so as to do away with the reproach of cold, calculating necessity. In the same way those who turn toward Christianity to gain an advantage try to become genuinely devout; because this will make the religious play-acting easier for them.

No standstill in love.—A musician who *loves* the slow tempo will take the same musical pieces more and more slowly. In the same way there is no standing still in any love.

Test of a good marriage.—The quality of a marriage proves itself when it can endure an occasional "exception."

Of the hour hand of life.—Life consists of rare individual moments of the highest significance and many countless intervals in which at best the shadow images of those moments hover around us. Love, springtime, a beautiful melody, the mountains, the moon, the sea—all these speak truly to our heart only once: if they ever in fact gain a voice. For many people never experience such moments at all but are themselves intervals and pauses in the symphony of real life.

Love as artifice.—If you really want to get to *know* something new (a person, an event, a book), you would do well to accept this new thing with all possible *love* and to quickly avert your eyes from everything you find hostile, offensive, false and even banish it from your mind so that, for example, you grant the greatest head-start to the author of a book and, as if watching a race with beating heart, you fervently desire that he may reach his goal. This process allows you to penetrate a new thing all the way to its heart as the place that actually moves it: and this is what is meant by getting to know it. Once you have reached this point, reason will afterwards impose its restrictions: this over-estimation, this temporary suspension of the critical pendulum was only the artifice for luring forth the soul of a thing.

Humanity in friendship and mastery.—"You go toward morning, so I will move toward evening"—to feel this way is the high mark of humanity in closer human relations: without this sensation every friendship, every discipleship and every student's relation toward a teacher turns at some point into hypocrisy.

Trust and intimacy.—A person who seeks assiduously to force intimacy with another is usually not sure whether he possesses that person's trust. If someone is sure of being trusted, he places little value on intimacy.

Advantage in deprivation.—A person who always resides in the warmth and fullness of the heart, as it were, in the summery airs of the soul, cannot imagine that tremulous joy which seizes winterly natures who are touched, for once, by the rays of love and the gentle breath of a sunny February day.

To let oneself go.—The more someone lets himself go, the less the others let him go.

Extravagance.—The mother of extravagance is not joy, but joylessness.

Bitterest error.—We are unforgivably insulted when we discover that in a place where we were convinced of being loved, we were seen only as household furniture and a piece of decoration that allowed the homeowner to display his vanity before his guests.

The shortsighted are in love.—Sometimes stronger glasses are sufficient to cure the lover; and whoever has the power of imagination to picture a face or a person twenty years from now would perhaps pass through life quite undisturbed.

To love the master.—The apprentice and the master each love the master differently.

To let oneself be loved.—Since when there are two people in love, there is usually one who loves and the other one who is loved, we have come to believe that in every love affair there would be a consistent quantity of love: the more one person seizes of it, the less is left over for the other. It happens very rarely that both of them are so vain that they each fancy *themselves* to be the one most deserving of love. In this way each of them now wants to be loved more by the other. In marriage, this state of affairs leads to some semi-comical, semi-absurd scenes.

Too close.—When we live too closely together with another person, what happens is similar to when we handle a good engraving over and over with our bare hands: one day we are left with nothing but a piece of bad and dirty paper. The soul of a human being can be similarly worn down by constant handling; at least it finally *appears* to us like that—we never again see its original design and beauty.—One always loses by overly familiar contact with women and friends; and sometimes one loses the pearl of one's life.

Love and hatred.—Love and hatred are not blind but dazzled by the fire they carry within.

A happy marriage.—Everything we get used to draws an ever tighter spider-web around us, and soon we realize that the threads have turned into ropes and that we ourselves are sitting in the middle as the spider that entrapped itself and has to feed on its own blood. This is why the free spirit hates all routines and rules, anything definitive and of duration, this is why, though painfully, he always again tears apart the net that surrounds him; even though he consequently suffers many small and large wounds—for he has to tear all of these threads *from himself,* from his body and his soul. He has to learn to love where until now he hated, and vice versa. Nothing must be impossible for him, and he must sow dragon's teeth on the same field where earlier he had emptied the cornucopias of his goodness.—All of this will reveal whether he is made for the happiness of marriage.

Love and honor.—Love desires, fear avoids. That is the reason why one cannot be loved and honored by the same person, at least at the same time. For someone who honors recognizes power, which means he fears it and is in awe. Love, however, recognizes no power, nor anything that divides, separates, elevates or denigrates. Because love does not honor, ambitious people are secretly or publicly recalcitrant to being loved.

Very heavy and heavy-hearted people will be made lighter and momentarily surface from their depths by love and hate, the very things that weigh other people down.

To discover that he is being loved in return should really sober up the lover about his beloved. "What? *She* is so modest as to love even you? Or so stupid? Or—or—"

Sensuality often bypasses the growth of love so that the root stays weak and is easy to tear up.

The chastest saying I have heard: "Dans le véritable amour c'est l'âme qui enveloppe le corps." [In true love it is the soul that envelops the body.]

Raising an objection, a short-lived affair, joyful distrust, and gleeful mockery are signs of health. Everything unconditional belongs to pathology.

Love brings to light the high and hidden qualities of a lover—what is rare and exceptional about him: to this extent, love easily misleads about his permanent traits.

The enormous expectation placed on sexual love and the shame attached to this expectation ruins any sense of perspective for women from the very start.

Here we need to invent new ideals.—It should not be permitted to make a decision about one's life while in a state of being in love, and to determine the character of one's company once and for all based on a heated whim: the vows between lovers should be publicly declared invalid and they should be refused the right to marry:—and this because we ought to take marriage unspeakably more seriously! So that in those cases where it had taken place until now, it would usually not take place! Are not most marriages of the kind that one does not want a third party to be a witness? But especially this third one is almost always there—the child—and he is more than a witness, namely the scapegoat!

Fear and love.—Fear has helped our general understanding of humanity more than love, because fear wants to discern who the other is, what he is capable of, what he wants: to deceive oneself here would mean danger and disadvantage. Conversely, love has a secret impulse to see in the other as much beauty as possible, or to elevate him to the highest possible position for oneself: to deceive oneself here would mean pleasure and advantage for love,—and so it does.

So love can be experienced as love.—We must be very honest with ourselves and know ourselves very well in order to practice this humane deception toward others, which is called love and goodness.

A test before considering marriage.—Granted she loves me, how annoying she would become for me after a while! And granted she does not love me, how especially annoying she would become for me after a while!—There are only two different kinds of annoyance—so let's get married!

Creating joy for others.—Why is creating joy for others greater than any joy? Because we thereby create joy for all of our own fifty drives at once. Separately they may each be very small joys: but if you put them all in one hand, then the hand is fuller than at any other time—and the heart as well!

Love and truthfulness.—Love turns us into inveterate criminals against truth, into habitual cheaters and thieves who allow more to be true that what seems true to us,—that is why the thinker has to chase away the people he loves from time to time (it won't be those who love him) so that they may reveal their sting and malice and stop *seducing* him. Accordingly, the thinker's kindness will have its waxing and waning moon.

To seduce to love.—The person who hates himself is someone we ought to fear because we will be the victims of his rancor and revenge. Let's see therefore how we can seduce him to love himself!

Love makes equal.—Love wants to spare the other to whom it consecrates itself any feeling of *strangeness*; consequently, it is full of dissimulation and approximation, it deceives incessantly and performs a sameness that in truth does not exist. And this happens so instinctively that women in love deny this dissimulation and constant, sweetest deception, boldly asserting that love *makes equal* (that would mean, it works miracles!)—This process is simple if one person lets himself *be loved* and does not consider it necessary to dissimulate, but rather leaves that up to the other, loving person: but there is no more convoluted and impenetrable performance than when both exist for each other in the throes of passion, and consequently abandon themselves, place themselves on equal footing and make themselves equal to the other and that other alone: and finally neither knows any longer what one is supposed to imitate, why one is supposed to dissemble, and who one pretends to be. The beautiful madness of this performance is too good for this world and too refined for human eyes.

Towards the light.—Men press towards the light not to see better, but to shine better. We are happy to accept as a light the one who makes us shine.

Two friends.—There were two friends but they had stopped being friends, and they undid their friendship from both sides at the same time, the one because he felt too misunderstood, the other because he felt too completely understood—and in this way both deceived themselves!—for each of them did not know himself enough.

You have to be secure in yourself, you have to stand bravely on your own two feet, otherwise you simply *cannot* love.

One must learn to love.—This happens to us in music: first one must *learn to hear* a figure and melody at all, to discern and distinguish it, to isolate and delimit it as a life in itself; then one needs effort and good will to *stand* it despite its strangeness; patience with its appearance and expression, and kindheartedness about its oddity.—Finally the moment arrives when we are *used* to it; when we expect it; when we sense that we would miss it if it were missing; and now it continues to compel and enchant us over and over and does not stop until we have become its humble and enraptured lovers, who no longer want anything better from the world than it and it again.—But this happens to us not only in music: it is in just this way that we have *learned to love* all of the things we now love. We are always rewarded in the end for our good will, our patience, our fair-mindedness, tolerance, and gentleness with what is strange, as it slowly casts off its veil and presents itself as a new, indescribable beauty—that is its way of *thanking* us for our hospitality. Even he who loves himself will have learned it this way: there is no other way. Love, too, must be learned.

"Selflessness" has no value in heaven or on earth; great problems demand *great love,* and only strong, well-rounded, secure minds who have a firm grip on themselves are capable of that. It makes the most substantial difference whether a thinker has a personal stake in his problems, so that to him they are his fate, his dire need, and also his greatest happiness, or whether he treats them "impersonally," which means that he knows how to reach and grasp them only with the tentacles of cold curiosity.

Feigning oneself.—She loves him now and gazes ahead with such calm confidence, just as a cow. Careful, now! What had bewitched him was precisely that she seemed utterly changeable and unfathomable! He already had too much steady weather in himself! Wouldn't she do well to feign her old character? To feign lovelessness? Isn't that the counsel of—love? *Vivat comoedia!* [Long live comedy!]

What do you love in others?—*My hopes.*

It is difficult to create in someone this condition of intrepid self-knowledge because it is impossible to teach love; for it is only in love that the soul gains the clear, discriminating, and despising view of oneself, but also that desire to look beyond oneself and to seek with all of one's strength a higher self that is still concealed somewhere.

The German philosopher Friedrich Nietzsche (1844–1900) considered it his task and vocation to take a metaphorical hammer to all of Western philosophy in order to expose how our morality and ethical beliefs are founded on falsehoods, repressed instincts, and manipulated emotions that parade as self-evident truths. This book is the result of reading Nietzsche's writings and much of the secondary literature over the course of thirty years—not as academic philosophy but as a guide to life. In Nietzsche's systematic critique of all of philosophy, *love* emerges as the experience that could let us escape the conventions and clichés that limit our lives.

For the philosopher who diagnosed the "death of God," transvalued all values, envisioned an *Übermensch* (superman) to overcome the decadence and nihilism he first diagnosed, and railed against the "herd mentality" of modern man, love has the potential to reveal ourselves to ourselves, or, in Nietzsche's deceptively simple phrase, "to become who you are." He presents many of his greatest insights in pithy, well-turned short phrases that prompt readers to think for themselves rather than follow a philosophical program step by dogmatic step.

Love, in Nietzsche's mind and experience, had been stripped of its radical dimensions and then corrupted by Western morality and religion in particular. By clearing away the sedimented beliefs that shape contemporary culture, Nietzsche discovers in love something that allows us to be ourselves despite the oppressive weight of civilization, and to be true to others as well. Love, for Nietzsche, is not the truth of our existence nor a solution to failed politics, but it harbors the potential for self-awareness that is the basis for the true recognition of others as well.

Nietzsche, the greatest ironist in the history of philosophy, anticipated that his work would be exploited to justify contradictory programs, from fascism to feminism, with enraged critics and equally passionate proponents on each side. He rails against readers who mine great books for nuggets of wisdom and ignore the rest, and pleads for slow reading—for readers who resist the compulsion for mastery, for figuring things out, for getting things done. You can't hurry love, as the song goes, and, as Nietzsche said long before, you can't hurry the truth.

This book was created in the spirit of slowing things down. Open this book anywhere and pause when a phrase or aphorism strikes an inner chord. Like love itself, this book ought to be a perpetual beginning and never the end. When a sentence or short paragraph speaks out to you, reread it, circle it, copy it into your phone, and close the book. It means that something in you spoke back to Nietzsche, and this type of dialogue—across time and culture, from one searching reader to one searching writer, heart to heart, mind to mind—is what philosophy should be all about.

Friedrich Nietzsche

Friedrich Nietzsche was born on October 15, 1844, the son of a Protestant minister and a minister's daughter in the town of Röcken (near Leipzig) in Germany, then Saxonia. His father was a talented musician but also suffered from mental problems, and upon his early death in 1849, Nietzsche lived with his mother and sister, Elisabeth, and enrolled in boarding school. As an ambitious student, he wrote musical compositions, poems and small books at an early age. At the University of Bonn and later in Leipzig, he studied theology and classical philology.

In 1869 he was appointed as lecturer and eventually Professor of Classical Philology at the University of Basel at age 24. Nietzsche's academic reputation and popularity with students suffered permanent damage from the severe criticism that followed his radical interpretation of Greek culture, *The Birth of Tragedy out of the Spirit of Music* (1872). He formed a close friendship with the composer Richard Wagner from 1869 to 1876, when Nietzsche finally broke with his famous mentor. In 1879, after struggling with persistent health issues, Nietzsche resigned from the university to become an independent writer. Periods of intense productivity would alternate with long travels to alleviate various health problems.

In 1882 Nietzsche met and fell in love with Lou Andreas-Salomé, a young Russian woman of extraordinary and unconventional intelligence. She declined his proposals of marriage but, for a time, the two remained friends. The efforts of Nietzsche's sister Elisabeth to sabotage their friendship led to a temporary break with his sister and mother. Nietzsche proposed to at least two other women but never married.

In 1885 Nietzsche's sister Elisabeth married Bernhard Förster, a rabid anti-Semite whose views shaped her later distortions, falsifications, and fabrications of her brother's writings.

After a brief period of mania in 1889, during which Nietzsche talked about his philosophical ideas and sent grandiose messages, he fell into a state of delusional and debilitating depression that rendered him essentially lost to the world. Nietzsche's mother was his caretaker until her death in 1897 at which time Elisabeth moved Nietzsche to the town of Weimar, Germany.

Nietzsche died on August 25, 1900, in Weimar.

In his lifetime Nietzsche published *The Birth of Tragedy* (1872), *Human, All Too Human* (1878), *The Gay Science* (1882), *Thus Spoke Zarathustra* (1883), *Beyond Good and Evil* (1886), *On the Genealogy of Morals* (1887), *Twilight of the Idols* (1889), among other books and essays. His last original book, *Ecce Homo,* was written in 1888 and published posthumously in 1908. While he was not regarded as a major philosopher in his lifetime, Nietzsche's ideas have exerted an immeasurable influence on philosophy, politics, art, literature, psychology, and popular culture around the world.

Sources

Giorgio Colli and Mazzino Montinari edited the *Collected Works of Friedrich Nietzsche* (Berlin/New York: de Gruyter, 1967 -), a selection of which is published in English by Stanford University Press. The present selection and translation is based on Colli and Montinari's *Kritische Gesamtausgabe*. A stable digitized text of that critical edition, incorporating all philological corrections for the print edition, is available at nietzschesource.org.

"Introduction to the Study of Classical Philology" (1871; lecture): 22.

Human, All Too Human. A Book for Free Spirits (2 volumes; 1878-1880): 1, 19, 20, 21, 28, 29, 30, 31, 32, 63, 64, 65, 67, 68, 69, 70, 72, 73, 74, 75, 78, 80, 81, 84, 85, 86, 87, 88, 89, 90, 91, 92, 93, 94, 95, 96, 97, 98, 99, 100, 117

Daybreak (1881): 39, 45, 67, 82, 83, 108, 109, 110, 111, 112, 113, 114, 115, 117

The Gay Science (1882): 50, 51, 52, 62, 119, 120, 121, 122

Thus Spoke Zarathustra (1883-1885): 3, 4, 6, 8, 9, 10, 11, 12, 13, 14, 15, 16, 17, 23, 25, 26, 27, 33, 34, 35, 40, 41, 42, 44, 55, 58, 59, 60, 61

Beyond Good and Evil (1886): 2, 38, 43, 48, 49, 71, 101, 102, 103, 104, 105, 106, 107

.

Contemplations

Great Minds on What Matters

SHAKESPEARE on Love
NIETZSCHE on Love
WILDE ON LOVE
RILKE on Love
DICKINSON on Love

Visit the
Warbler Press Contemplations series at
warblerpress.com